MINER:
12 THINGS TO KNOW

by Samantha S. Bell

STORY LIBRARY
MORE TO EXPLORE

www.12StoryLibrary.com

12-Story Library is an imprint of Bookstaves.

Developed and produced for 12-Story Library by Focus Strategic Communications Inc.

Library of Congress Cataloging-in-Publication Data
Names: Bell, Samantha, author.
Title: Miner : 12 things to know / by Samantha S. Bell.
Description: Mankato : 12-Story Library, 2022. | Series: Daring and dangerous jobs | Includes bibliographical references and index. | Audience: Ages 10–13 | Audience: Grades 4–6
Identifiers: LCCN 2020015782 (print) | LCCN 2020015783 (ebook) | ISBN 9781632359414 (library binding) | ISBN 9781632359766 (paperback) | ISBN 9781645821069 (pdf)
Subjects: LCSH: Miners—Juvenile literature. | Mineral industries—Juvenile literature. | Work environment—Juvenile literature.
Classification: LCC HD8039.M6 B45 2022 (print) | LCC HD8039.M6 (ebook) | DDC 622/.8—dc23
LC record available at https://lccn.loc.gov/2020015782
LC ebook record available at https://lccn.loc.gov/2020015783

Photographs ©: Mark Agnor/Shutterstock.com, cover, 1; ironwas/Shutterstock.com, 4; Arthur Greenberg/ Shutterstock.com, 5; Magdawszedobylska/CC4.0, 5; Adam Ziaja/Shutterstock.com, 6; iurii/Shutterstock.com, 7; Sumit buranarothtrakul/Shutterstock.com, 7; Vladimir Mulder/Shutterstock.com, 8; Albert Russ/Shutterstock.com, 9; Hugo Infante/Chilean Government/UPI/Alamy, 9; Vladimir Mulder/Shutterstock.com, 10; Tyrol5/CC3.0, 11; Alice Nerr/Shutterstock.com, 12; I Made Pasek/Shutterstock.com, 13; Peter Righteous/Alamy, 13; David Levenson/ Alamy, 14; Greenshoots Communications/Alamy, 15; Photopat/Alamy, 15; ironwas/Shutterstock.com, 16; Joe Baraban/Alamy, 16; SeventyFour/Shutterstock.com, 17; Cultura Creative/Alamy, 18; King Ropes Access/ Shutterstock.com, 19; John Robinson/Africa Media Online/Alamy, 19; Sunshine Seeds/Shuttertock.com, 20; desdemona72/Shutterstock.com, 20; LeventeGyori/Shutterstock.com, 21; King Ropes Access/Shutterstock.com, 21; Cultura Creative/Alamy, 22; U.S. Labor Department/Alamy, 23; Bascar/Shutterstock.com, 24; marcos alvarado/ Alamy, 25; Frank Heinz/Alamy, 25; Fredy Thuerig/Shutterstock.com, 26; Bennian/Shutterstock.com, 27; Alice Nerr/ Shutterstock.com, 27; Luke Schmidt/Shutterstock.com, 28; Dmitry Kalinovsky/Shutterstock.com, 28; pan demin/ Shutterstock.com, 29; cemT/Shutterstock.com, 29

About the Cover

Miner working with underground equipment.

Access free, up-to-date content on this topic plus a full digital version of this book. Scan the QR code on page 31 or use your school's login at 12StoryLibrary.com.

Table of Contents

Some Miners Work above Ground

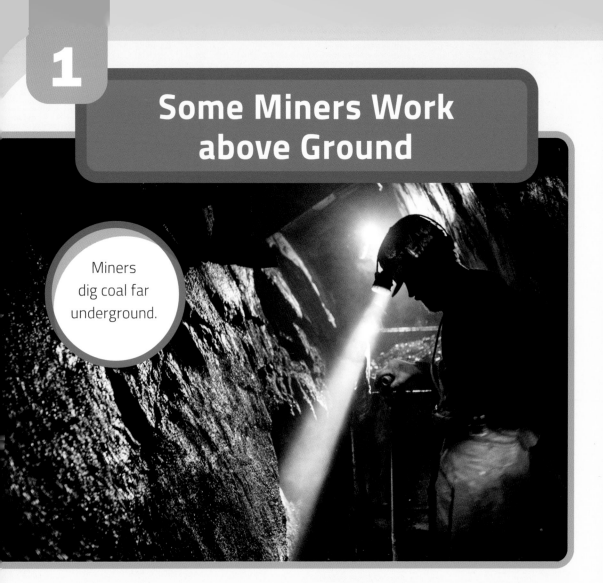

Miners dig coal far underground.

Mining is the removal of rocks and minerals from the Earth. But not all miners work underground. Many work at mines on the surface, too.

Underground mining is used for minerals that are deep down. But sometimes the minerals are closer to the surface. Pit mining removes some of these. Placer mining removes minerals from the sediments in rivers and streams. It also removes them from beaches.

Open pit mining removes minerals near the surface.

FIRST DISSOLVING, THEN REMOVING

Some miners work in in-situ mining. This method of mining is used for getting and removing uranium. First, a drill goes down into the rock. Then the uranium is dissolved using a special mixture of water, oxygen, and carbon dioxide. It can be brought to the surface without moving any other rocks.

The type of mining used depends on several things. One of these is the location of the mineral deposit. Another factor is the strength of the rock. Cost for mining the mineral is considered, too. Once the mine is established, the miners get to work.

Sulfur is taken from the volcanic soil on Mount Ijen in Indonesia.

$82.2 billion
Value of nonfuel minerals produced in US mines in 2018

- Some mines are located near communities.
- The communities are often small towns.
- The miners and their families form strong friendships.

2

Mining Machines Can Be Dangerous

Miners use many different tools and machines to get the job done. Some tools are electric. Others are powered with air. Some use fuel. Miners work with drills, power shovels, and loading machines. They use cranes, rail cars, and conveyor belts. Accidents can occur. Sometimes miners come in contact with the equipment. They may become severely injured. Many times, the accidents are fatal. Thousands of miners die every year from mining accidents.

Some accidents are avoidable. Vehicles can be equipped with sensors or other warning systems. Other improvements include tracking devices. These monitor the positions of

workers and hazardous equipment. Improvements in communication help, too. That way, officials can keep track of where the miners are. They can make sure they are safe.

THINK ABOUT IT

Accidents can happen with all kinds of machines. What machines do you use? What steps do you take to stay safe?

340

Amount in tons (580 metric tons) that a loaded haul truck can weigh

- Large mining vehicles and other heavy machinery have blind spots. Those are areas around the vehicle that the driver can't see.
- They can crush smaller vehicles.
- Backup cameras help keep drivers and passengers safe.

3

Cave-Ins Trap Miners Underground

Sometimes mines collapse. Miners can be trapped underground, inside the mine. Sometime they are even killed. Tremors in the ground can cause a mine to fall in. Earthquakes cause these tremors. So do explosives that the miners are using. Miners use explosives to break up the rocks. Tremors can also come from the mine itself. In 2007, long tunnels in a mine in Utah acted like cracks in the Earth. They produced tremors and a cave-in.

Even metal supports do not always succeed in holding up the mine walls.

22
Number of miners trapped in a cave-in in China in October 2018

- The miners were working in a coal mine in the Shandong province.
- Pressure inside the mine caused the rocks to break.
- Only one miner was saved.

Old fashioned wooden supports often collapsed.

Sometimes mines collapse because the wooden supports are not strong enough. They also may not be properly secured. As mines go deeper, the weight of the ground above increases the pressure. That pressure can cause the floors, walls, or ceilings to fall in.

The Chilean miners were trapped underground for 69 days, but all were rescued.

SURVIVING UNDERGROUND

In August 2010, a mine in Chile collapsed. Thirty-three miners were trapped 2,300 feet (700 m) underground. The miners had a little food and water in a shelter in the mine. Rescuers worked for more than two months to reach them. All 33 miners survived.

4

Water Can Flood a Mine

Both underground and above-ground mines are at risk of flooding. Sometimes too much groundwater comes in. Run-off from heavy rains can also flood a mine. Some mines are dug near aquifers. An aquifer is a layer of rock that holds groundwater. If the ground near the aquifer is damaged, the water can flow into the mine. Floodwater

Many underground mines are below water level and flood if not continually pumped clear.

9

Number of miners trapped in the Quecreek coal mine in Pennsylvania

- In July 2002, water broke through a wall and flooded the mine.
- The miners were trapped for over 77 hours.
- Rescuers drilled an escape shaft into the mine. All of the miners got out.

Statue of miner to commemmorate Quecreek mine rescue.

settles into the lower areas of the mining tunnels.

Flooding can cause a lot of damage. It can make the walls of the mine unsteady. They may collapse. Flooding can also block the escape routes, trapping the miners. To prevent flooding, miners use a system of pumps to get the water out. Levees can also help keep water out of surface mines. The levees help hold the water back. They are often built in flood-prone areas.

11

5

Explosions Are Deadly

Many types of mining involve explosives to remove materials.

Underground coal mines are most at risk from explosions. Methane is released when coal is mined. Explosions can occur when there is a buildup of the gas. A small amount of heat can cause it to explode.

Coal dust also causes explosions. Methane is easier to set off than coal dust. But coal dust produces more pressure and heat. The explosions are much bigger. Sometimes a methane

Underground fans help extract methane and other dangerous gases.

PREVENTING EXPLOSIONS

Fresh air helps reduce the risk of explosions. Large fans can blow air in or out of the mine. This reduces the amount of methane in the air. The fans must be kept in good working condition.

explosion will set off a coal-dust explosion.

The heat that ignites the gas or dust can come from many different things. It may be an open flame. But it can also be an electrical spark from a machine. It can start with just a hot surface.

9.5

Percent of methane in the air that is the most dangerous, the "perfect oxidation point"

- In November 2010, the Pike River mine in New Zealand exploded.
- Officials believed the explosion was caused by a buildup of methane gas.
- Twenty-nine miners died.

6

Mining Dust Causes Lung Disease

Both surface and underground miners can develop diseases from dust. Surface miners can get silicosis. Silica is a mineral found in the Earth's crust. When rocks are crushed, they produce silica dust. Sometimes surface miners breathe in the dust. The lungs become scarred. The miners have trouble breathing.

Underground miners can get black lung disease. Known as silicosis, it results from breathing in the silica in coal dust for a long time. Coal dust is made of tiny particles of silica. These settle in the lungs. The immune system tries to remove the dust particles. This can lead to scar tissue in the lungs. Black lung

Dust and smoke are hazards of mining.

disease can cause a cough or shortness of breath. It can even lead to heart failure or lung cancer. There is no cure for silicosis or black lung disease.

THINK ABOUT IT

Can you think of anything else that causes lung disease?

16

Percent of coal miners in the US who may develop lung disease

- Black lung disease can take years to develop.
- Sometimes miners don't have any symptoms until after they retire.
- There is no cure for black lung.

All that dust and smoke can destroy lungs.

Miner Earnings Vary

The amount of money a miner earns depends on several things. These include the size of the mining company. It also depends on how long the miner has worked for the company. The type of job makes a difference, too.

The location of the mine also affects how much a miner earns. In the US, miners

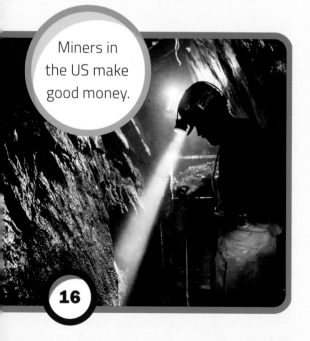

Miners in the US make good money.

make about $55,000 a year. But in some other countries, they can earn much more.

16

Mining project managers have enormous responsibilities.

Australia has a shortage of miners. The average salary there is around US$95,000 (A$136,000).

In many places, miners do not need a lot of education. For example, in West Virginia, many coal miners do not have a college education. Some did not even finish high school. But the starting salary for a coal miner there is $55,000 to $60,000.

Generally, the highest paid person in any mining operation is the project director. That individual can earn more than $400,000 a year.

$102,100
Average annual mining salary in Alaska in 2018

- Alaskan miners are among the highest paid in the US.
- There are often few jobs available in rural Alaska. The mines offer job opportunities in these areas.
- Approximately 4,500 people work in the Alaskan mining industry.

Some Mines Are Too Hot

Deep underground mines are hot and humid. One reason is because of the heat from the rock itself. As the mine gets deeper, the temperature rises. Groundwater flows through the hot rocks. Then the water becomes hot and evaporates. It transfers the heat into the air and increases the humidity.

Mining activities such as drilling, blasting, and welding release even more heat. Engines, motors, and other equipment create heat. So do the miners themselves.

Sometimes miners suffer from the heat. The first sign of a heat-related illness is heat cramps. This is when the

Massive machines mean massive heat underground.

Miners must wear protective gear despite the fierce heat underground.

muscles contract. Heat cramps are painful. But they usually last only a few minutes. When miners don't drink enough water, they can get heat exhaustion. The symptoms include headaches, dizziness, and vomiting. Heat stroke is even more severe. If it isn't treated, the miner could die.

140°

Temperature in degrees Fahrenheit (60°C) in the world's deepest gold mine

- Mponeng is a mine in South Africa. In 2018, it was approximately 2.4 miles (3.9 km) deep.
- The mine has an unusual cooling system.
- Tons of ice slurry is pumped into underground reservoirs. Giant fans help spread the cool air.

Noise in Mines Causes Hearing Loss

Loud machines contribute to hearing loss for a miner.

Mines contain high levels of noise. The heavy equipment creates a lot of noise. Drilling does, too. All of this noise is confined to a small area. As a result, many miners suffer hearing loss. The mining industry has one of the highest rates of noise-induced hearing loss.

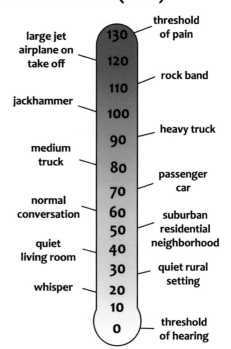

Decibel Scale (dBA)

Sound	dBA	Reference
	130	threshold of pain
large jet airplane on take off	120	
	110	rock band
jackhammer	100	
	90	heavy truck
medium truck	80	
	70	passenger car
normal conversation	60	
	50	suburban residential neighborhood
quiet living room	40	
	30	quiet rural setting
whisper	20	
	10	
	0	threshold of hearing

The noise in mines can lead to other health problems, too. These include ringing in the ears. It can cause high blood pressure and headaches. The noise can also make workers feel tired or stressed.

Employers are required to keep the noise levels below 85 decibels. When it goes higher, they need to provide the workers with hearing protection. Eighty percent of the miners in the US are exposed to this level of noise.

Hearing loss from noise happens over a long period of time. Workers usually don't realize its effects until after their hearing is damaged. This type of hearing loss is permanent. It can't be reversed.

90
Percent of coal miners over age 50 who have hearing loss

- Hearing loss from noise is preventable.
- Workers need to be educated on how to prevent it.
- They also need protective equipment. Earmuffs and earplugs must be a good fit.

Miners Need Special Training

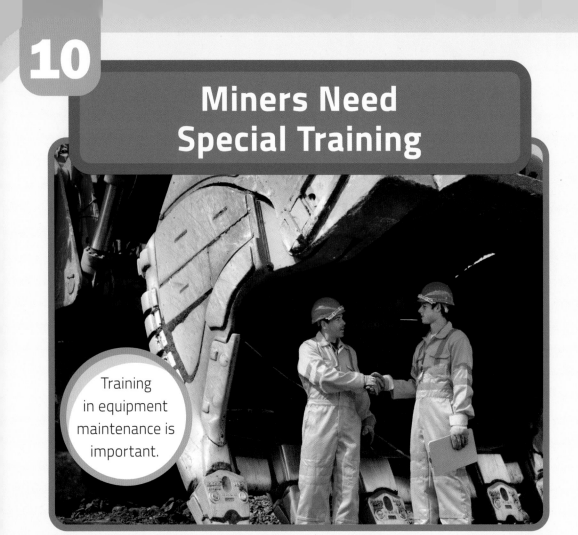

Training in equipment maintenance is important.

People don't need a lot of diplomas and degrees to become miners. But they must take special classes. Miners need specialized skills. Some miners operate and maintain the machines. Others calculate where holes and cuts will be made. Some miners lay track. Some install equipment that prevents cave-ins. Others design and carry out blasts with explosives. Training also helps miners work more safely.

The law requires that all miners receive basic and refresher training. The safety training

THE MINE SAFETY AND HEALTH ADMINISTRATION (MSHA)

The MSHA develops and enforces safety and health rules for US mines. It provides training and educational programs for mine operators. These actions help to reduce the number of injuries, illnesses, and deaths that occur in mines in the US.

The MSHA trains mine operators and workers.

24

Number of hours of training a new surface miner is required to have

- After completing the training course, the miner receives a certificate.
- The miner gives the certificate to the employer as a record of the training.
- Surface miners also need eight hours of a refresher class each year.

required depends on the type of mine where the person works. It also depends on how much experience the miner has.

Some Mines Have Deadly Gases

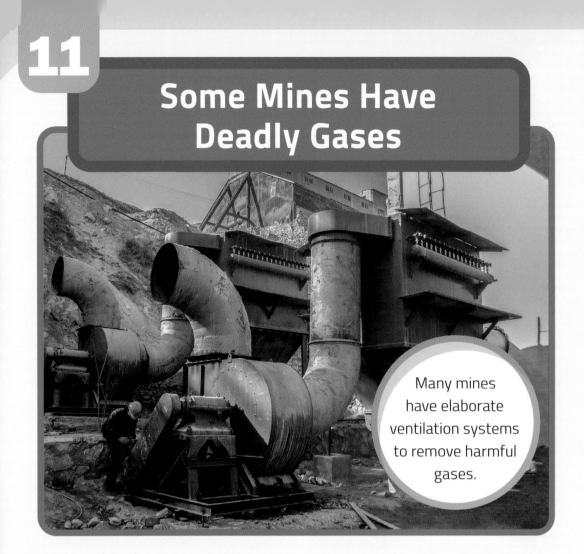

Many mines have elaborate ventilation systems to remove harmful gases.

A mine can have a danger in the air. The air may contain poisonous gases. Sometimes there may not be enough air to breathe.

Hydrogen sulfide is a poisonous gas. It smells like rotten eggs. It can form when water in the rocks reacts with the minerals. For example, it may be found in old pipelines or stagnant water.

Carbon monoxide is a colorless and odorless gas. It is also poisonous. It is used to put out fires by releasing it into the air. It can even affect workers who are far away.

Sophisticated ventilation systems remove harmful gasses.

Carbon dioxide is another gas found in mines. Coal that is in contact with the air uses oxygen to produce carbon dioxide. This gas can replace the oxygen in the air. Then the miners don't have oxygen to breathe.

The air underground is limited. The gases do not have anywhere to go. That is why a good ventilation system is so important. That way, the toxic gases don't build up.

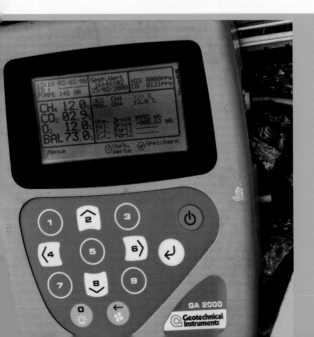

1986
Year miners stopped using canaries as a warning system

- Miners took caged canaries into the mines with them.
- Too much carbon monoxide made the birds fall from their perches.
- Today, modern equipment measures the gas.

Miners Look for More than Coal

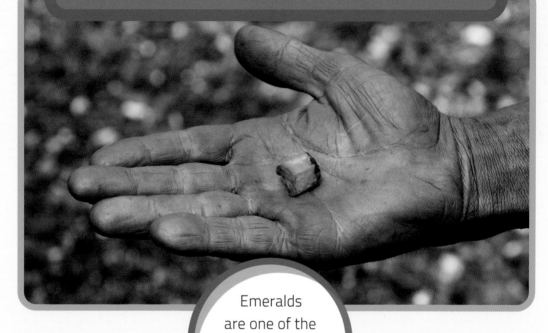

Emeralds are one of the most highly prized gemstones in the world.

Mining involves searching for metals, minerals, and rocks in the earth and bringing them to the surface. The materials that are mined depend on where the mine is located. For example, mines in China produce the most gold. They also lead in producing silver, copper, and zinc. US mines produce the most lead. US mines also produce minerals such as beryllium and cobalt.

Gemstones are minerals chosen for their beauty. They can be cut and polished. Some are worn as jewelry. There are many different types of gemstones, including diamonds, rubies, and emeralds.

Some miners dig for coal. Coal is a combustible rock found

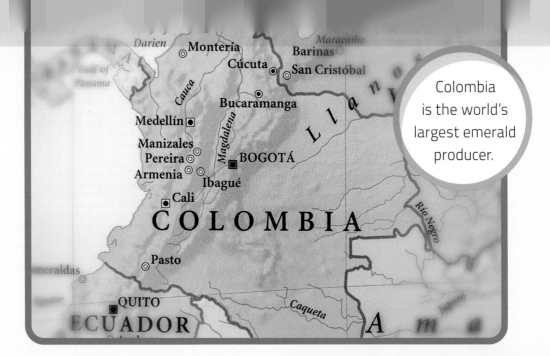

Colombia is the world's largest emerald producer.

around the world. It is used to produce electricity. Layers of coal can be found between layers of rocks. Some of the largest coal mines are found in the US, Australia, and China.

THINK ABOUT IT

What kinds of rocks or minerals can be found where you live?

35

Approximate number of countries where diamonds have been discovered

- The top diamond-producing countries include Russia, Botswana, and Congo.
- The largest rough diamond was found in South Africa in 1905.
- It was called the Cullinan Diamond. It weighed 3,106 carats (621.3 g).

An open pit diamond mine in Russia.

More Daring and Dangerous Jobs

Demolition Blaster

A demolition blaster detonates explosives to destroy structures. They may be bridges or buildings. The blaster must figure out the best and safest way to bring down the structure.

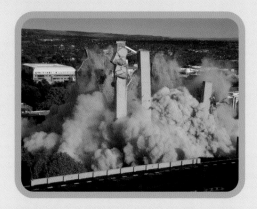

Underground Construction Worker

Underground construction workers build tunnels and other passageways beneath Earth's surface. They face many dangers, including the risks of fire, explosions, and polluted air.

Oilfield Worker

Oilfield workers perform jobs that take oil from the ground. They may be exposed to hydrogen sulfide, a toxic gas often found in areas drilled for oil. High amounts can cause immediate death.

Mine Rescue Worker

Mine rescue workers move into action when an accident occurs in the mine. Sometimes they work in contaminated air or water. They may have to put out fires underground.

Glossary

contract
Tighten or shrink, becoming shorter in length.

combustible
Substance that can catch on fire and burn easily.

decibel
The unit used to measure the loudness of a sound.

flood-prone
Any area that is easily and frequently flooded.

groundwater
Water that is beneath Earth's surface, held underground in the soil or rock crevices.

humidity
Level of water vapor, or moisture, in the air.

immune system
The system in the body that protects it from infection from foreign substances, cells, and tissues.

levee
An embankment built to prevent flooding.

methane
A colorless, odorless gas that can easily ignite and is often used as a fuel.

slurry
A semi-liquid mixture consisting of fine particles in water.

ventilation
Fresh air provided to an area such as an underground mine.

Read More

Alkire, Jessie. *Coal Energy: Putting Rocks to Work*. Minneapolis, MN: ABDO Super Sandcastle, 2018.

Aronson, Marc. *Trapped: How the World Rescued 33 Miners from 2,000 Feet Below the Chilean* Desert. New York, NY: Simon & Schuster Atheneum Books, 2019.

Farndon, John. *Rocks, Minerals, and Gems*. Richmond Hill, ON: Firefly Books, 2016.

Martin, Claudia. *Rocks, Fossils, Minerals, and Gems*. London, UK: Quarto QED Publishing, 2018.

Visit 12StoryLibrary.com

Scan the code or use your school's login at **12StoryLibrary.com** for recent updates about this topic and a full digital version of this book. Enjoy free access to:

- Digital ebook
- Breaking news updates
- Live content feeds
- Videos, interactive maps, and graphics
- Additional web resources

Note to educators: Visit 12StoryLibrary.com/register to sign up for free premium website access. Enjoy live content plus a full digital version of every 12-Story Library book you own for every student at your school.

Index

About the Author

Samantha S. Bell has written more than 125 nonfiction books for children. She also teaches art and creative writing to children and adults. She lives in the Carolinas with her family and too many cats.

READ MORE FROM 12-STORY LIBRARY

Every 12-Story Library Book is available in many formats. For more information, visit **12StoryLibrary.com**